REAL ESTATE INVESTING FOR BEGINNERS IN 2020

A PROVEN GUIDE TO MASTERING PROPERTY MANAGEMENT EFFECTIVELY

By

Alan Matthews

Disclaimer

Disclaimer and Terms of Use: The Author and Publisher has strived to be as accurate and complete as possible in the creation of this book, notwithstanding the fact that he does not warrant or represent at any time that the contents within are accurate due to the rapidly changing nature of the Internet. While all attempts have been made to verify information provided in this publication, the Author and Publisher assumes no responsibility for errors, omissions, or contrary interpretation of the subject matter herein. Any perceived slights of specific persons, peoples, or organizations are unintentional. In practical advice books, like anything else in life, there are no guarantees of results. Readers are cautioned to rely on their own judgment about their individual circumstances and act accordingly. This book is not intended for use as a source of legal, medical, business, accounting or financial advice. All readers are advised to seek services of competent professionals in the legal, medical, business, accounting, and finance fields.

Description

There isn't really an entire library of great real estate books out there. Anyone who is really interested in reading only the best, need to spend an entire day, or two to read from the best resources.

What you won't find as often, is a coherent, executable, business plan detailing what it takes to get going with real estate investing as a beginner.

If you want to venture into real estate investing, what you really need is a book that lays everything out, from A to Z, with what to do at every step along the way.

This book however, is one of the best you will get out there. It covers a wide range of real estate investing for beginners.

It incorporates all you need to know about real estate.

This book enriches you with an in-depth understanding of the benefits of real estate, and how profitable it can be in the year, 2020. It gives a detailed explanation on how to become a property manager.

It goes deep and wide into answering almost every question you may be having about Real Estate Investing from different angles, to make you have a full understanding of why real estate investment is the most profitable.

The content of this book includes;

* A guide to real estate investment for beginners
* Learning the basics of real estate investing
* Steps for successful real estate investing for beginners in 2020
* How to evaluate an investment property
* Resolving the real estate investing fear factor as a beginner
* Mistakes to avoid in real estate investing

And a whole lot more.

At the end of this book, you will have the knowledge on how to make better real estate investment in 2020.

Table of Content

CHAPTER 1

INTRODUCTION TO REAL ESTATE INVESTING FOR BEGINNERS

If you're looking for new ways to make a living or just a few bucks on the side away from your regular job. You should consider real estate investing. A lot of people are intimidated by the thought of going into something new. Their thoughts usually follow along these lines:

Too much to learn.

High startup costs.

There's nobody to turn to, for help.

It goes on and on. There are no shortages of excuses for not starting a new venture. While they all sound reasonable, these excuses serve no purpose other than to prevent you from taking actions.

Thinking of starting something new?

Real estate investing can become very profitable for those who know what they're doing.

What is Real Estate Investing?

Real estate investing involves the ownership, purchasing, rental, management and sale of real estate for profit purpose. Improvement and Development of realty property as a component of real estates investment strategy, is commonly viewed as a sub-specialty to fame of real estate contributing called real estate advancement.

Real estate investing in 2020 and beyond offers great opportunities, but investing in real estate successfully will be no walk in the park. Real estate investing before the financial crisis was smoke and mirrors. Now, investing in the market is akin to stock investing. There is no sure thing. Investing for beginners can be very tricky.

As a beginner in real estate investing, when you start the search for information on real estate investing for beginners, you'll find that there are a lot of experts and mentors out there looking to sell high priced information. You also get some offline resources at the library, and bookstore. Maybe you'll even find someone who's out in the trenches on a regular basis and is willing to take you out on the streets to show you some of his properties.

The real estate investment is the most rewarding, and fast developing investment market, but one need to select the right time to invest in this market. This market provides budding investors with the most successful business opportunities for investment.

For those who know what they are doing, real estate investing in 2020 will become very profitable. You can make a huge profit from real estate investing in 2020. For those who don't really know what they're doing, real estate investing can start to feel like a bad idea.

Real estate investing for beginners isn't totally different from real estate investing. All things being considered, you're all trying to accomplish similar goals; get a decent profit for the properties you purchased. Figuring out how to get that profit is the secret to success in real estate.

For beginners, it's ideal to get familiar with everything you can, before you start investing. Real estate isn't difficult to figure out, and the more information you get, the more cash you stand to gain from your real estate investment.

Real estate investing for beginners should begin with a lot of studies. You need to study the market, study the properties that are available and accessible in your vicinity, study the public reaction. This implies that you should invest little time and energy simply watching properties in your vicinity. Get to know what is selling, what is not selling, and where these properties are located. Success at real estate investing frequently depend on where and what properties you purchase. A good-looking home in a terrible neighborhood won't sell just as it would in an extraordinary neighborhood, and your investment is what will suffer. You need to know which location/area is popular, and which zones have properties that don't sell too. Real estate investing for beginners means taking time and effort to learn all you need to know about real estate, before you go right into spending.

Keep in mind that for beginners who are just getting into in real estate, it's always good to seek assistance from experts. You should speak to real estate agents, speak to contractors, and above all, speak to other real estate investors. Learn all you can from these people. This way, you can learn the secret to success in real estate investing. Real estate investing for beginners is just like any other real estate investing, only with little experience.

It's very important that when in real estate investment, you give buyers what they want. Real estate experts will say "it's the kitchen and bathrooms that make or break the sale of a house", this is because, in homes, it's the kitchen and bathrooms that make the most impact on potential purchasers.

Giving people a pleasant property is very important, this is because they won't want to buy anything they might consider sub-par. If you wouldn't want to buy the property, chances are good that no one else will want to buy too. And if no one purchases, then you have made a poor investment, and will probably end up losing the entire investment. The truth is, a property that won't sell is worthless to real estate investors.

The Location is one of the most important factor. Depending on this, one can visualize appreciation of the property. In case of buying land, one need to go for land near the highway. Buying a land far from the city may not get much appreciation. When there is an economic recession, and property prices fall, it is the right time to invest in real estate. You can get prime property for throwaway prices.

Real estate investment depends on budget and the nature of the project. Accordingly, one can go for bank loan or ask a developer for flexible payment options.

Getting the property with all the amenities promised by the builder and on time possession of the property are most important. One should get the completion certificate from the buyer which is helpful, if one wants to sell off that property. Clear title of the property where the construction is taking place is also very important. New buyers/investors should be careful about getting attracted by fake promises. One must get all property-related documents thoroughly checked by the respective government authority and an attorney. This gives the proper financial safety.

Real estate investing, even for beginners, is not extremely complicated. But, it can be challenging. Although, what you need is to learn a few of the ABCs of real estate investing. This basics can help you succeed in the market. Once you start, you may never want to stop.

CHAPTER 2

LEARNING THE BASICS

As said in the previous chapter, real estate investing for beginners is not extremely complicated. But, it can be challenging. However, if you know where to start, and how to press the right buttons, everything can be easy.

You want to go into real estate investment, but don't know where to begin, consider yourself luck. Because, regardless who you are, you can go into in real estate investment. Real estate investors are making five figures, monthly net profit. You should know that investing in real estate does not require using your own money. You can use someone else's money. What do you bring to the table? Your skills and knowledge.

Real estate investing for beginners incorporates a couple of interesting factors to consider before choosing your first property to purchase, and deciding to enter the market. You have to understand that many people have lost money by making the wrong decision. The key to profiting in real estate is to buy when market prices are low, and sell when they are high. You should realize some significant hints to consider before you decide on your first property, and enter the market of real estate investing.

One of the things to consider about investing in real estate property is the location. At the point, when you are contemplating which property you need to get, you have to consider the locations that may be expected to become popular sooner or later, but with a price which has not gone up yet. This might mean they are situated on the outer parts of town, or they might be situated near a planned resort area. When you are looking at property to invest in, think about whether the chances of it going up will be better than some other locations for real estate investing.

You might want to consider investing in real estate that is priced lower than market prices. You can find good deals on property that the owner needs to sell, because of a job transfer or divorce. This might mean that you can get the property for lower prices than other homes in the area, and you will have better chances of making a profit when you sell. You might find a property that needs a few repairs or just needs a coat of paint and some minor details added. These can be the best chances to make better profits when you start real estate investing.

Another thing to think about is finding property that can be rented out to make the mortgage payment. If you pay the right price and get the right financing for the real estate you buy, then you can afford to rent it until the market goes up, and you can make a profit. Keep in mind that you will need to find a good renter, and pre-screen them to find ones that pay their bills on time and will not damage your property. You do not want the added expense of hiring a lawyer and evicting renters that have not paid rent or caused damage, but this can be part of real estate investing.

If you need a mortgage on the property you invest in, you need to make sure there is no penalty clause for paying the loan off early. This can happen if you buy property and fix it up to sell quickly. You can make a profit this way, but if you have a penalty for paying off the loan early you might have to pay an added two or three percent of the mortgage when you sell it. Many bankers understand that you plan to fix up the property and sell it, but they may require a higher down payment if they know you are real estate investing.

Consider ways to save money on closing costs, and real estate fees. You can get better deals when you discover property available for sale by owners, because they are saving the agent fee. These fees can be 7% to 10% of the property price. But, it is a fee that is paid by the seller. Many investors always use agents because they can help them find the best deals. The main thing to consider is that you get the best price on the property and do not pay over market price when you are investing in real estate.

Do not make these common mistakes when investing in properties;

Think carefully before you make offers on properties, and do not rely on gut instincts, because they are not always right.

Make sure you do your homework on properties before you invest, and find out as much as you can.

Inspect the properties for major defects, and consider a professional home inspector.

Do not rely on rumors or promises about a certain area becoming popular or prices going up, because of plans to develop it.

Do not become emotionally involved with properties because it can cause you to make bad decisions that cost money when you are real estate investing.

How exactly do you ensure making it big in real estate investing?

Through the years, many have become millionaires and billionaires through real estate investing, and it will even be more profitable in 2020 as the number of people purchasing properties have been increasing by the year. The year 2020 will definitely not be an exception. However, it can't be over emphasized that irrespective of the increase in property ownership, some still fail in real estate investing, and end up losing a huge amount of money to nothing. The business can be very tricky, and if you are not keen enough to learn the trends, and tricks, you might end up losing all your funds. There is more to being a property investor, than just closing, and collecting money. One effective approach to increase your chances of being successful in real estate investing is by learning the basics. Consider the following tips before you go into real estate investing to earn the income that you deserve:

1. Spend money before you make it: Real estate investing for beginners can be a bit tedious. It is true that real

estate is profitable. However, be prepared to spend much before you even make your first sale. All business requires spending, and real estate investing isn't an exception. There is a wide range of expenses that you need to be mindful about. This includes; licensing exams, business license, fees, and so on. You need to have at least, a half year savings ready for unforeseen expenses in the future.

2. Flexibility: One of the reasons why many people want to give the industry a try is because, they want to leave the routines that come with their regular jobs. However, if you are a new property investor, you should be ready to invest much time while starting out. You need to keep in mind that money does not come easy with real estate. In fact, most investors work at night, weekends or holidays. Your client might want to look at the house during their leisure time, which usually falls on weekends and holidays.

3. Play Safe: You should know that you will be spending time with people whom you haven't met before. Keeping yourself safe should be paramount. Aside keeping yourself safe from your market, you also need to keep yourself safe from scammers, who pretend to

be real estate mentors. These people pretend to sell materials online, but they are simply scammers, who want to rob you of your money. Safety is a very important factor that needs to be strictly considered by every beginner.

What Every Real Estate Investor Newbie Needs To Know

- You will have to trade time and money to get what you want in real estate. The saying "You can't get something for nothing" and "nothing goes for nothing" comes into play in real estate investing. So, even if you buy an expensive course to get someone else's experience, and shave years off your learning curve, you'll still have a learning curve. Also, you'll need to find leads, and that type of marketing takes time, and money.

- Leverage cuts both ways. At that point, when the market is booming, leverage can be an incredible partner in helping you acquire more property with less of your own cash. However, when the market is declining, as this also happens with real estate market cycles, having a great deal of leverage can put you down on your value and income. Protect yourself by profiting when you purchase, and leaving behind those thin deals.

- It's all about negotiating with the motivated sellers. A lot of courses make you believe that if you find motivated sellers, you can just strike a deal like daisies in the orchard. That's almost true. Whether you're working in commercial or residential real estate, you'll get much better deals when you negotiate with a motivated seller. However, the key is that you must negotiate. You have to make offers that will work for you, and you have to find sellers that you think will be motivated, and offer them your low cash offer or terms offer, to see if they're willing to work with you. Engage them in long conversation by making lots of offers, and negotiating with the ones that are motivated.

- You get paid for solving problems. Real estate investing is a business with a lot of problems. Sellers can get very emotional, or have a lot of financial trouble at the time that you'll be working with them. That's stressful for anyone, especially when the transfer of a large asset like a house, apartment, building or office/retail center is involved. Realize that you may go through some challenging emotions of your own. That's natural. If you can hold it together, and survive the up and down roller coaster, you should do just fine.

- Get to know your rate of return. When you don't have a deal, it's easy to think that any deal will be good. However, sometimes the best deals are the ones you pass on. You make your cash by saving yourself from some costly mistakes. Try not to waste time on property that doesn't make sense when you run the numbers. Don't get emotionally attached just because someone says they're motivated or willing to work out terms with you. Run the numbers. Always focus on the numbers.

Real estate investing can offer some great returns, but there's a reason not everyone goes after them. Not every property is a winner. Finding and acquiring the winners can be a challenge. However, if you are committed to making your real estate investments work for you, then focus on getting yourself educated and staying in for the long run.

With respect to the market, if you find a seller willing to sell for less than 20 percent of the market value, then you should purchase. Purchasing bargain real estate is probably the most ideal approaches to profit. If you make an offer, ensure you know how much the property will be worth once you've done the repair/fixup, in case you intend on flipping the house to raise capital. It is a wise idea to choose a specific geological zone and work it exclusively. So, you become a guru on what houses are selling for. That way, you know how much benefit is to be made when you sell.

Don't give up! Make a ton of offers with various properties available. There are always deal properties hanging tight for brilliant investors. Don't ever forget that.

If you follow these basics, then you should have no issue kick-starting, and profiting with real estate investing. Remember that it takes time and hard work to make it pay off.

The fast rising costs of homes across the world over recent number years has gotten many people's attention. In fact more individuals are interested in pursuing real estate investment. Real estate can be a very tricky market, not something you need to engage in except if you have some great knowledge and experience.

Maybe you have some idea of what kind of property you would like to invest in, the most important factor in your decision should be the appraisal. This step is so important that it is worth your time and money to hire a professional with a lot of experience in property appraisals. The appraiser is trained in analyzing the property and its surrounding local market to come up with the estimated value. A common misconception is that appraisers create value, but in reality they interpret the market to estimate a value. They will consider things like the size of the property, its location, the amenities, and the condition of the structure, just to name a few. Having a property appraised is a simple advice, but it truly gives you an idea as an investor, if the investment is worthwhile. You would hate to sign the papers only to find out the market is not what you expected, or that the property actually has some faults that will decrease the value you recover from it.

In addition to have the property appraised, it is important to be able to forecast the entire local market as an investor. You must look at a market and decide if it is profitable or not. One indicator that most investors will consider is the average time a house is on the market in that area. If homes are selling fast, and their average market time is low, this is a good sign that the market is hot, and could be profitable. Another statistic to take into account is the difference between the initial asking price, and the final sale price. If there is a huge difference, there is a good chance that the market is soft and not favorable for an investor. On the other hand, if the average sale price is close to asking price, the market is likely strong.

The home or property that you are interested in is no doubt the focus of your investment research, but there are other factors that will influence the success of your investment. Often, people will buy a home only to find out later that a huge shopping mall is being planned at the backyard. Others have had similar problems with multi-lane roads being put in or in California, homeowners have had to fight to keep casinos (and it's associated traffic) out of their neighborhood. Not all future constructions is bad. Maybe there are plans for a church, business park or school close to you. Before making a purchase it is wise to head down to city hall to look into any future land use plans that are in the works for near your investment property. As you could imagine from the above examples, changes in land use near your home or investment can drastically alter its value. It is better to be aware of these things prior to investing.

Another piece of advice you must always keep in mind is that tax laws change. As an investor, you must be well aware of real estate tax laws. The laws are going to change all the time, it is your responsibility to stay on top of these changes. Some investors feel they can handle staying abreast of the changes, while others don't have that kind of time. So, they hire a tax law attorney to help them. It is important not to solely rely on tax laws to make your investment worthwhile. A good investment will always be a strong investment no matter the changes in the law. Being knowledgeable of the latest tax law will allow you to benefit maximally from your investment.

There are a lot of things to consider when investing in real estate, most of which are common sense. Experience will definitely give you the best guide into the real estate investment market. As a beginner, it is essential to get your feet wet without making mistakes that result in huge losses. If you are just getting started remember these tips: have the property appraised, judge the market yourself, become an expert on real estate tax laws, and plan for the unexpected. With these things considered you should be on your way to becoming a success as a real estate investor.

CHAPTER 3

OPTIONS AVAILABLE FOR BEGINNERS

Real estate investing is not as scary as you think. The truth is, real estate investing for beginners is not as scary as most people think it is. In fact, it should be the opposite. Real estate investing is an easy, affordable, and very profitable way to make money. The most amazing part of real estate investing is that you can make cool money from it, and still go on with your regular job.

Real estate investing is an excellent method of building massive fortunes. You should know that you need to have other stable means of injecting cash for financial stability while doing real estate deals.

There are various options available for you if you are considering it as an investing means. I see no reason you shouldn't though. Most wealthy people in the world have one way or another gained their wealth through property investing. With this, comes the risk associated with the property investing.

You should decide where you like to start your trip into this lucrative business. Just don't forget that after you've begun your investment career, it is highly recommended to use more than one type of investment methods to diversify and spread the risks, as this is a precarious market at its finest.

You can learn to make a fortune from real estate investing by this few methods. The following are just several methods of real estate investing, together with their associated risks.

1. **Owning Rental Properties**

   Buying and holding onto rental properties is a great way to make a fortune. Nothing beats regular fixed income from rentals monthly, and annually. The best online courses will show you how to buy, repair, and rent properties by following a proven formula.

2. **Commercial Real Estate**

   Buying a commercial property is a good place to start. It is relatively secure when compared to several of the other forms of real estate investing. The problem with commercial real estate is that it is a huge investment to start with (it involves a lot of money). This is something that many real estate investors don't even think until they have built a sizable portfolio, and have plenty of money to risk. It is stable because most businesses that lease from you will seek to lease on a long-term basis. Businesses prefer to stay in one location as long as possible, because it's bad for business in most cases to frequently move, they tend to stay a while.

3. Flipping Homes

Flipping homes is becoming a popular form of real estate investing, and many people have learned that this is also a good way to quick profit. This is a high-risk business to say the least, but the rewards are equally huge when a flip goes well. You need to decide if you are ready to take the risk as house flips are part skill, and part luck. It's easier than you think.

4. Residential Investment Rental Properties

Becoming a landlord is not as having business properties, or flipping highly profitable properties for quick cash. It is a good method to work out for a comfortable retirement. Residential investment rental is a long-term kind of real estate investment. However, the profit can be worth when all is done accurately.

5. Pre-Construction Real Estate

This method is considered more risky than house flipping in various ways. Particularly, as it has become so predominant in current years. The secret key with this kind of investing option is searching for the right property in the right market place. If you can invest in a city that will have a serious housing scarcity, or is in beginning stages of housing shortage (for example, some desert and coastal areas have encountered in previous years), you might just get the fortune you seek. The highly competitive and highly speculative natures are the issues of this investing option.

6. Lease to Own

Lease to own properties often bring great benefits. For a number of property owners, this is preferred than straight up renting for several reasons. One, the individuals who are planning to own their homes are more likely to take good care of their homes as compared to those who are merely renting. This implies that, if for some reasons they choose to move elsewhere and do not complete a lesser amount of payment, the probability of requiring major repairs before you can accept another client is little. You have the option to ask a little more than rent, applying a small percentage of the monthly rent to the purchase price or down payment of the house. You can also be helping a family that might have encountered rough time along the way to get the dream of home ownership.

7. HUD Wholesaling of Homes

This is a variation on the house flipping process. The best HUD house wholesaling experts use a special system for offering, buying, and then selling HUD properties.

These methods are just a few of the more popular methods real estate investing for beginners can turn novice into a successful real estate guru. Follow these methods, and before you know it, you will be the expert everyone goes to for the real estate secrets for making huge money.

Where to Start For Beginners

Learning the basics of real estate investing can be a bit complicated. You can only learn the process gradually. Below is what you might need to kick start.

- **Signing Up For Extra Classes**

Attempt locating an affordable, credible classes on real estate investment. These classes should be taught by specialists who specialize in real estate investing. This will help you a lot because you will be dealing with experts in person. It is important that you know the significant bits of legislation concerning real estate, since you can't generally depend on others to do so for you. Certain purchasers and sellers may try to exploit you, or may lead you to break the law unknowingly due to lack of knowledge. There are also clubs for people interested in investing in real estate. Join one of these, so you can learn practical things from more experienced investors.

- **Learn How to Make a Proforma**

The term "proforma" has many meanings, depending on the field and context in which it is used. Often, it refers to something that people just do because it is a formal or bureaucratic requirement, even though it does not serve any real purpose. In real estate. However, the meaning is somewhat different. Basically, a proforma is a document you draw up to gauge whether a certain investment project will actually help you earn money. You should learn how to do one for a project, so you will know if it is actually worthwhile investing in that enterprise. Luckily, you can find templates for this document online and basically fill in the blanks with the appropriate amounts. Of course, gauging the appropriate amounts is easier said than done, which means you should also do some investigating into the costs of construction, renovation, and other processes.

- **Thoughts and Feelings**

Investing in real estate may appear to be an entirely intellectual, practical interest. However, beliefs and feeling play major part in the types of investment you can effectively make. This is particularly true once you really sell or lease the property. You should work with individuals whose interest clash with yours, so you should realize how far you are set to go to secure a decent profit on your investment. For instance, if a buyer with a big family and limited funds wants to buy your property at a very low price, will you have a hard time pushing for the price, you need to make your venture profitable? If you decide to rent or lease out the property but the tenant is unable to pay rent, will you be willing to evict him or her and find another tenant who is able to pay? Would you prefer to get a property manager to handle such things, and if so, can you afford a trustworthy one?

CHAPTER 4

A GUIDE TO REAL ESTATE INVESTING FOR BEGINNERS

New real estate investors can either be blindfolded or have narrow vision. There are numerous errors to be made in real estate that has left many without a shirt or nickel in their pocket.

Here are some considerations to go through before you start your investing business.

First, start with the end in mind. What are you looking to get out of investing? OK money is a given, but what kind of money?

There are three types of income you can make through real estate investing;

    i.   Quick upfront lump sum cash

    ii.   Passive income, and

    iii.   Create long-term wealth.

Depending on what is it you want to accomplish, you will then determine on what kind of strategies, you will pursue to reach your goals.

If you are looking to get lump sums of cash, then you should be looking into fix and flips and wholesaling. Lease options may be a possibility if you are also looking to combine passive income to your strategy.

If you are looking for passive income, then you should look into multi-family dwellings and other cash flow properties. Even commercial real estate could be part of your agenda, but this is more advanced. As a beginner, you should probably master residential first unless you have a wonderful mentor for commercial.

To build long-term wealth, you should follow a buy and hold strategy which is kind of interesting to talk about during this recession, but know, there are many places where this strategy works. Depending on your strategy, you may have to go to different cities to invest.

Understand that the laws will vary from state to state and will have to adjust your acquisition strategies. Whether you are buying through auction, short sales, land contracts, equity sharing, options, notes, etc. you must keep in mind the end goal.

With the end goal in mind, you will also be able to decide upon the right legal entities to form and how you choose to be taxed. Your lawyers and tax advisors should help you with that.

Estate planning also plays a part, so make sure you get personalized help. There is no such thing as one size fit all. I guess this is the reason many make mistakes, there's so much left unconsidered.

Things You Can Do To Become Successful in the Real Estate Industry

- **Build Your Subject Competence**

  As a real estate investor, you need to learn the basics of the business.

  As a real estate investor, you don't need to be a geek. However, you should at least know your craft and master its fundamentals. You should also know the many ways you can profit from property acquisition. Another important lesson to be learned is to master the timing of one's cash flow.

Investors should learn various evaluation techniques to figure out if a certain piece of property is best suited for one's investment agenda. Investors also need to at least learn some of the most basic real estate laws in the places where they wish to do business.

- **Get First Hand Experience**

The most fundamental approach to benefit from real estate investing is via rental property. That will involve taking on the role of a proprietor or a landlord. Make sure you try out what it's like before actually investing some of your capital on certain properties.

One good example of getting your feet wet is to get a job as a property manager. This will give prospective entrepreneurs that firsthand experience in dealing with tenants, managing and maintaining properties, and all the gritty details of managing a piece of real estate property with the idea of making profits

- **Learn Other Ways to Invest**

There are actually other ways to invest in real estate other than acquiring the basic rental properties. Investors can look into leveraging, investment trusts, trading (flipping), and investment groups among others.

How to Evaluate an Investment Property

Investing in real estate can be very complicated. You know you want to invest in something that will yield a solid return on investment, and you want to generate income on a regular business, so choosing real estate is a good plan. How can you evaluate a property to see if it will be a good investment?

One of the things you likely are searching for is to realize riches without putting in great deal of additional work. Your life is full enough as it is. This is where doing your homework upfront will spare you a ton of time and effort. Something else to keep in mind is that property, unlike other types of investments, is not a liquid asset, meaning you can't convert it to cash quickly. It will benefit you to consult with an adviser who can guide you to properties that will realize a positive rate of return. A property that looks really good but doesn't actually give you cash out of it is not worth your time and money.

To get started, you should look for properties that are ready to go. Anything that qualifies as a fixer upper or base land that does not have anything developed on it are not places a beginner should consider. Established buildings can give you an immediate return and steady cash month in and month out.

Be sure you do your homework on the property first, before investing in it. Check with your city development office or your county planning division to find what you can about the history of the property, and make sure you get a thorough inspection. It might look really nice from the outside, but there may be some significant damage that is hidden from view. As your first investment property, steer clear if you find structural issues - they're just too costly to repair and recoup your costs on.

A nice clean place on the other hand, will allow you to start leasing it right away. Long term tenants mean steady income for years to come. Regular maintenance will keep the property in good condition, and you can spend a minimal amount of time managing your investment. You can also hire a property manager to handle all of the day to day operations and maintenance, and make your investment even more stress free. Just remember that this will cut into your profits.

If you are looking into buying a fixer upper that you can renovate and flip for a profit. Look for one in a good neighborhood. Established areas near good schools are great places to start looking. Homes in good condition that are being sold as estate sales are ideal, because the house will more than likely just need a freshening up with some modern appliances, and perhaps some new paint. Once again, be sure you have a good inspection done just to ensure that the house itself will be in good overall condition.

Getting into the real estate investment business shouldn't be done alone. Having a partner like a real estate agent or an adviser will protect both your interests, your assets, and leave you free to enjoy your investment.

Myths of Real Estate Investing

Most stories of real estate are based on the idea that goals and fortune should be accumulated and enjoyed more quickly than in other areas of investment. But real estate investing is a business, and like any other business it takes time and perseverance to grow and prosper.

Below are some of the myths of real estate investment.

1. **Real Estate investment doesn't work.**

   There are many individuals who don't have the foggiest idea where to begin or who to ask with regards real estate investing.

In the past years, a lot of new investors flooded the real estate market, lured by tales of immediate fortunes. Some subscribed to online courses chockfull of "secrets" or attended one day seminars to learn "everything there is to know." Others made phone calls to Realtors, demanding to be shown some investment properties. These approaches lack focus, education, and commitment. Therefore, they do not bring success. Effective investing takes a well-coordinated arrangement explored by an experienced group, devoted to meeting short and long term objectives. If you are focused on doing the fundamental work, it can work for you

2. **Real Estate investing is for those who are only good in doing business.**

Most people are afraid of trying something new or don't want to appear foolish. Take note that every expert was once a novice. Every millionaire had his first deal. There is no such thing as a magic touch, but there is education, effort, and experience. Many avoid success because they are afraid to ask for help. While being the newbie is often frightening and disheartening, you can target the right people to talk to, prepare your questions, and set yourself up for success, making the process more manageable and less intimidating.

3. Real estate investment is risky.

Unsafe as it might appear, investing is just as risky as the investor. One of the significant reasons we center around the need to fabricate a personalized investment is to confine the risk. No transaction, no deal, and tax duties ought to be handles without the whole team in play. So, to be a successful investor, the person who maximizes return while constraining losses, you must have authorize specialists directing your portfolio. Such rules will lessen your risk, and keep your business on track.

4. Real estate investing is very time-consuming.

I completely empathize with this problem. Time management is one of the hardest strategies to master. We have to make some tough decisions about our time. Some make great sacrifices regarding leisure time, creature comforts, and holiday spending. For you to be successful investors, you have to take a look at what commitments were obligations and what activities were negotiable. You may have to take some tough choices in the future.

5. **Real estate investing involves lots of fixing.**

We have heard so many capable individuals scoff at being a land lord, because they don't want to fix a clogged toilet at 3 a.m. surprisingly, we don't know anyone who has ever had to do this. The chances of this ever actually coming up are slim, especially when you are being proactive with repairs and upgrades can keep your property low maintenance. Besides, you can always hire a property manager to call on if an emergency situation arises. Don't let this myth prevent you from making additional money and benefiting from tax advantages.

6. **It's hard to know where to start in real estate investing**

Perhaps your credit is a mess, and you just don't have the time to deal with it. Maybe everyone you know lives paycheck to paycheck, and you're not sure who could lead you in the right direction. Whatever the reason, it no longer has to hold you back. There are reliable resources, reputable organizations, and numerous facilities available for new investors.

CHAPTER 5

RESOLVING THE REAL ESTATE INVESTING FEAR FACTOR AS A BEGINNER

If you have thought about real estate investing, but yet to kick start fully due to the phobia that the market might collapse once you step in, and you will lose all your investment. You know what? You are not alone.

There is this fear factor in every new investor, and no one successfully investing today will say otherwise. It's very common for potential real estate investors to miss out on extra ordinary opportunities for an overwhelming sense of fear.

Okay, so let's address some of the most common fears, and see whether we can help you to become less anxious, and maybe take the plunge into real estate investing after all.

- **Negative Cash Flow**

The thought behind investing in real estate is to make enough cash to cover working costs, and advance installment with some left over to save in the bank. Having to nourish a property won't cut it, no financial specialist needs to feed a rental property.

In all honesty, this fear might be the easiest to manage on the grounds that is very straightforward. Just run the numbers before you purchase. Get the property's last one year income and working costs, calculate a mortgage payment, and fit the results into a spreadsheet or real estate investment to determine the cash inflow income. If the cash inflow is negative, so be it. Otherwise, disperse the concern and push forward.

Simply utilize sensible rents, a vacancy rate (regardless of whether the owner claims full occupancy), working costs (remember substitution holds), and a loan payment to compute your yearly income.

Never simply work away because the property shows a negative cash inflow. Dig dipper, and look for ways to manage the cash inflow. Numerous rental income properties just go negative because of poor management, you may have a probability of raising rents and cutting working costs. Who knows, you may considerably find an opportunity overlooked by the present owner.

- **This Isn't the Right Time**

Truly, for any number of national or international events, potential investors frequently feel it is worthwhile to hang tight for better times before making an investment in real estate.

But little do they know that real estate investment has little to do with the economic climate at the time they purchase. Foremost, consider the long term, economic depressions come and go, but how will the investment property impact your future rate of return? That is what matters.

If this helps, remember that unlike the fluctuating stock market, real estate has a significant record for steadily increasing in value. Maybe not overnight, and not without an occasional bump. Yet, real estate worth increases over time.

- **Losing Your Money**

Obviously, you wouldn't want to tap into your reserve funds to make perhaps the biggest financial investment of your life just to end up losing everything.

The key is to study and research. Find out about the property you want to invest in, and the location you intend to invest. Search for sources of information like college courses, real estate software, seminars and real estate investing books. Get a specialist evaluation of the property from an investment real estate expert or property appraiser. There is always some risk in real estate investing, but developing a plan with enough information will negate majority of your uncertainties.

- **Tenant and Management Hassles**

  Okay, it's true. No one wants the headache of having to repair a refrigerator or to fuss with an unruly tenant, and it is understandable why that concern does prevent many people from becoming real estate investors. But life is always a series of tradeoffs, and trading off an occasional migraine for potential future wealth is generally worth it.

  However, it's also true that in time you will learn to deal with and manage most issues in your sleep. If not, you can always hire the services of a reliable property management company to deal with it for you. The advantage being that it will relieve you of the time and stress of having to deal with tenants, repairs, and in turn puts matters like late rents into the hands of experts.

- **Lack of Real Estate Experience**

  Just because you have not yet purchased an investment property should not keep you from real estate investing. In this case, locate a real estate agent who specializes in investment property to assist you.

  When the time actually comes to buy a rental income property, you'll be surprised to discover that it's not as insidious as it looks, and tapping into the mind of an expert will increase your comfort level significantly. But the keyword here is investment property specialist. A real estate agent who just sells houses won't benefit you, you need a real estate professional with true real estate investment experience.

- **It's Time to Get Started**

  The hardest part about going into real estate investing is getting started. We're great at making excuses, and there are always numerous reasons to put off starting something new.

  Yes, we want to be cautious. It's better to approach real estate with adequate knowledge. So if you're struggling, here's a suggestion; learn, research, and plan. Educate yourself about real estate investing, learn about real estate in general, and more specifically about your specific real estate market. Develop a road map about the financial security you hope to achieve.

Afterward, pick out that first rental property, make a purchase, and then take over as manager. If you are stuck to your investment plans, work diligently to increase income and control expenses, in time you'll be able to move on to bigger and better properties.

After all, that is the nature of real estate investing.

STEPS FOR SUCCESSFUL REAL ESTATE INVESTING FOR BEGINNERS IN 2020

I f you are interested in real estate investing, here are step plans anyone can use to invest in real estate.

1. **Create an Investment Plan**

   Everyone needs an investment plan to be successful in real estate investing. This plan is an outline of the investment, and should include a number of components. A successful investment plan will include purchase strategies, clearly defined goals, and contingency plans for any possible events or change in circumstances. Having all of these planned out can ensure a successful investment. The success or failure of these investments may be dependent on the underlying plan that is followed.

2. **Choose an Investment Philosophy**

   Investing in real estate can be made possible in various ways. Foreclosures are prominent target for investors, and flipping homes is common in the housing market for a profitable investment. It is crucial to pick which philosophy to put your resources into before starting any real estate investment. Recognizing these components will enable the investor narrow in on these segments for better investment results.

3. **Find/Choose your market**

Finding your market means finding your target area, the geographical location of where you want to purchase real estate. Ideally, it's best if you purchase property within 10 to 20 mile radius of your home. The closer you are to your investment property, whether it's a house, mobile home, or vacant land, the better.

Choosing your market will be determined by the amount you can make, known as the Return On Investment (ROI), minus your expenses when you sell or rent the property. And your ROI will be affected by a number of factors-current market values of the existing properties in this area, upcoming developments planned for the area, proximity to landmarks or bodies of water, crime rates for the area, employment opportunities for the area, and a lot more.

Visit the area at night. During the day, an area with a few abandoned houses or commercial buildings may appear like an opportunity. At night however, these buildings may be a haven for criminal activity or a camp for homeless people. Talk to the people that live in the area to get a feel for what's going on there.

4. Choose your investment property type

What type of real estate property are you trying to put resources into?

How would you want to purchase this investment property? Buy it out rightly, or set up the initial installment on it to secure the mortgage. Securing the mortgage of an investment property enables you to set aside cash while, also getting control of the property.

5. Collect the Required Financial Resources

The next step for successful real estate investing is to gather all of the financial resources that will be needed to make this investment possible. This may mean gathering together cash, or some investors may choose to obtain pre-approval for a home loan, so that any offer can be backed up with proof of fund availability.

6. Establish a back-up plan.

Just what it says. Set up a plan in the event that everything goes wrong, in case of a situation in which everything goes south. Establish a contingency plan. You've made it this far, now make a backup plan. You can do it.

Making a backup plan will lessen any worries you have, enabling you to move forward, to take action, to make things happen. Action eliminates fear.

7. Determine your exit strategy

You first need to decide where you want to end up in order to know where you are going. What's your end target? How do you plan to exit this RE deal with an attractive profit, and with all parties (purchasers, sellers, investors) satisfied and happy?

So as to know where you are going, first choose where you need to wind up. What's your ultimate objective? How would you intend to leave this RE manage an attractive benefit, and with all gatherings (purchasers, merchants, financial specialists) fulfilled and cheerful?

8. Present your plan to investor or investors

Read over your notes and reduce everything to a simple plan of action. Then, write down this plan of action and reduce it to numbered steps... 1, 2, 3 and so on. Set the dates of when you're going to do what. Make copies of this, both PDF copies and hard copies.

Get everything in writing, signed, in the presence of a notary public.

9. Execute your plan

Take action. Action eliminates fear.

Start putting your plan into action by taking action.

10. Interview and Assemble a Team of Professional Service Providers

To be successful in real estate investing a team of professionals is usually needed. This can include a home inspection company, a real estate broker, an attorney, an accountant, and an insurance agent as well as other professionals who may be needed. These team members can provide valuable advice and services, and prevent some of the most common real estate investment mistakes.

11. Learn Everything Possible about Housing Market

Knowledge is the best way to succeed at any investment, and this is true in the real estate market as well. Learn as much as possible about housing market. Make research about the real estate market in your locality and learn about home values and regular styles in the area. If the objective is to flip homes or fix up properties and lease them out in that case learning about common repairs and related costs is also a good idea.

12. Put your exit strategy into motion

Collect rents, sell the property, and keep records of everything (video, audio, paperwork, keep backup paperwork).

13. Find Properties and Make an Offer Contingent on an Acceptable Inspection Report

Once a suitable property has been located then it is time to make an initial offer. This offer should always include an inspection clause and time period. Neglecting to include this clause could end up costing an investor any possible return on the investment if there are hidden defects or undisclosed problems.

14. Get people competing to buy your property

When selling or renting the investment property, gather a crowd by scheduling a specific time. If you want to rent or sell a property, set up a specific time frame in which to show the property, preferably on the weekend. Schedule an open house on Sunday, 2pm - 4pm, gather a big crowd. Get a mortgage broker at the place to0, in order to set up mortgages for people who want the place.

15. Negotiate An Agreeable Price And Close

This step in the real estate investing process for many individuals is to negotiate the final price, and then close on the property. If the property is to be flipped then it will need to be renovated before being sold. Other investors will make any needed repairs, and then rent out the home instead.

CHAPTER 7

HOW TO MAKE BETTER REAL ESTATE INVESTMENT IN 2020

Individuals who have gone into real estate investing knows that if the investments are made well, one can get profitable returns without much stress. There are a lot of approaches to earn significant profits real estate investing. If you feel that the place where you have invested beneficial, you can gain an attractive amount of profits.

For a beginner in real estate investing, there are a lot of challenges to encounter. However, if one is able to take the chance and is mentally prepared to bear the responsibility and risk, there is definitely a lot to earn and much to learn. However, in the long run, when one has gotten some experience, he can become a real estate expert closing a series of rewarding real estate deals.

You need to acquire few skills beforehand if you want to be succeed in the field of real estate investing come 2020. This skills can help you be a real achiever in real estate investing. There is a couple of skills required for investing in a real estate deal, which are obligatory for a profitable real estate deal.

These skills include;

1. Learn to find serious sellers

You should be aware of how and when to find the right sellers. Finding serious sellers is one of the basic skill you need to learn to thrive in real estate investing. These sellers can help you to earn reasonably in the real estate. Make sure the sellers are of high repute, as if you are investing for the first time.

While you are a beginner, you attempt to acquire the abilities of how to manage real investment issues. It is very important to procure high degree of skills in shutting down real investment deals.

2. Gain expertise in all the fields revolving around the real estate investment

In order to gain expertise in the real estate investment field, you must procure skills in all the other fields that revolves around real estate investing. You must also be aware of the language and terms used in the real estate investment world.

3. **Ability to analyze real estate investment deal perfectly**

This is another important skill you need to acquire. If you are able to analyze the real investment deal, you will be able to figure out where, how and when to deal. This will help you profit in the long run, as you will be able to calculate the risks and benefits to some extent.

If you are able to acquire all these, then there is a high possibility that you will thrive in real estate investing in 2020 and beyond.

Real estate investing for beginners includes some important concepts regarding the amount of capital available to invest and the earnings desired to make the investment worthwhile.

While these figures are solely subjective, and can completely differ from instance to instance. There are primarily two types of investments to be considered in 2020. They are;

Value Added Investments and Value Driven Investments.

Value added investments are going to provide more significant returns. Particularly in the long run, since the risk is usually higher. A standard value added property will produce a 12% to 25% return on investment depending on exactly how long it takes to optimize its value.

Value driven investments are secure financial commitments backed by constant leases with intermittent rental increases which will give you a return in the 6% to 14% range based upon the demographics, marketplace, age of investment, tenants' credit rating, etc. These properties will generally become more competitively priced the larger they are as institutions will compete for the larger ones (over 100,000 square feet).

Since institutional purchasers require a reduced return, they will undoubtedly propel the price up to a point where it's no longer advantageous for a smaller buyer. I generally advise focusing on properties which can generate in excess of a 10% return, meaning that both you and also the investors can make money.

Another significant concept to be considered by new real estate investors in 2020 is "the significance of utilizing leverage". Leverage is the utilization of obtained funds to finish an investment transactions. The higher the proportion of borrowed funds used for investment, the higher the leverage. Thus, the lower the amount of equity.

I suggest that on value driven investments you use no greater than 70% leverage. However, in value added investments, you can put on as much as 100% leverage hinging on just how quickly you can actually do the things which are going to increase the value.

Taking these concepts into consideration will help you determine what kind of property will meet the parameters required to achieve your financial objective.

If you uncover a property that meets or surpasses your criteria and you desire a loan, present it to a bank or a mortgage broker who will usually shop it around as well as find you some basic quotes. You can then ask them to issue you a letter of intent setting out the terms at which they will be able to provide a loan to you.

Getting a clear idea from a lender on how much your monthly mortgage payments will be will help you determine how much cash you need to invest and what your cash on cash return will be. And this should ultimately help you decide on whether or not you should buy a particular property.

As you can see, real estate investing for beginners can be easy when the questions about the investment are resolved in advance of any potential acquisition. Careful preplanning that is well thought out will result in successful investing.

Is Real Estate a wise Investment for 2020?

Is the real estate a good investment for 2020? YES!

With 2020 drawing closer, you should consider the most ideal way to invest in the New Year. There are a lot of investment systems, including residential real estate properties. So which one would it be? Real estate investing in 2020 is not only a wise investment, but one of the best things to invest in. You are wondering why?

Here are reasons why Real Estate investing is a wise choice in 2020 and beyond.

Before we go through the reasons, United States of America housing market forecasts for 2020 which make real estate stand out among other investment choices. Let's have a have quick look at the general advantages.

4. **Wise investments are low risk.**

All investment hold a certain level of risk, the best investments to make enough money tend to be a relatively low risk, at least relative to the rate of return that they offer. This is actually the situation with investing in investment properties. As real estate properties are substantial resources, it is impossible to simply lose everything as a property investor. If the overall U.S housing market or the local real estate market go through a recession, it is bound to come back. People will definitely need a rough over their head. So real estate demand is guaranteed to be there. The fact that real estate is a low risk strategy makes it a wise investment in 2020 and beyond.

5. The best investments discourages inflation.

The motivation behind people in all over the world ponder over where to invest their money is to protect it against inflation. Else, they would keep it in the bank where it's very safe. The value of properties in real estate rises overtime, and this is known as natural appreciation. The fundamental driver behind this phenomenon is the fact that the land on which the real estate properties are built is a limited resource, coupled with the consistent increase in population which puts more weight on the interest for housing. Without a doubt, the normal yearly rate of real estate appreciation has surpassed the average yearly inflation rate in the U.S housing market in the previous decade, and this pattern is expected to continue in 2020 and beyond.

6. Investing for revenue is essential.

The most ideal approach to invest should provide investors with money in the long term and short term. Rental real estate properties enable a real estate investor to start making money immediately. When he/she is done purchasing an investment property, this property can be leased quickly to begin generating monthly rental revenue and return on investment. That is why investment properties are often referred to as income properties. With real estate investing technique, you don't need to wait for years for your assets to appreciate. Moreover, you can choose how to profit in real estate for the greatest return.

7. Profiting in the Long Term is Important.

Pondering over where to invest to get great returns over the long run? The answer is real estate once again. As mentioned above, real estate appreciation happens naturally, without any effort for the benefit of the investor. This means with private investment properties, you can make tons of cash passively once you choose to sell your home. So, if that is not a wise decision, what is?

8. Real Estate Investing for Beginners Is a Reasonable and Viable Option.

Many of the best investments are hard to get started in as they require extensive knowledge and understanding of the market. Besides, many of them require full time commitment so as to produce the best return on investment. This is certainly not true about real estate. First of all, you don't need any particular degree if you are thinking of how to become a real estate investor. All the knowledge and information that you need is available online. Purchasing investment property with great investment property with great top rate and money return doesn't involve detailed expertise or manual real estate market analysis and investment property analysis anymore. In 2020, the best real estate investment tools allow investors to find a profitable income property for sale in a matter of minutes.

To invest in real estate, you don't need to leave your 9 to 5 job. With the help of software tools and professional property management, you can make passive real estate investments on a part-time basis.

So, you see why real estate investing is great in general. But how about in 2020? Will it be the same case?

Why Real Estate Remains a Wise Choice For 2020

To answer this question "is real estate a good investment in 2020?" We need to consider the U.S housing market trend expected for 2020.

These are the most important factors which both experienced, and beginner real estate investors should keep in mind for 2020;

9. Real Estate Prices Will Keep Going Up

Speculations that the real estate might go into another downturn in 2020 are just speculations. There are no signs to show that this will be the case. On the contrary, the vast majority of real estate experts expect the values of homes available for sale in the housing market to keep expanding at a lower rate. If you are beginning to think whether investing in a rental property for sale is worth it in 2020, be rest assured that it is. The slowdown in the rate of real estate appreciation is any time in the near future. Moreover, only a small decline in the appreciation rate is expected, while real estate prices will really keep rising quicker than the inflation rate.

10. Absence of Affordability Is Not a Defining Factor

Many real estate specialists including real estate investors keep worrying about the growing lack of affordability in the housing market. However, this is not a constraining issue in the general market, but more of an isolated issue in certain markets. It is obvious that purchasing an investment property in location such as San Francisco real estate market, the Los Angeles real estate market, and the New York estate market is challenging. Particularly for those just getting into real estate investing. However, other places like the Dallas real estate market offer more reasonable and affordable real estate listings. With the right tool, new real estate investors can easily find income properties at sensible costs with great cap rate and great return. All in all, purchasing cheap properties is still suitable possible in many locations, which is one of the reasons real estate is a good investment strategy in 2020.

11. Interest Rates Are Expected to Remain Low in 2020

Experts predict that interest rate will keep being relatively low at around 4 percent in 2020, which implies that those who are worried about how to invest in real estate due to insufficient capital can resort to a mortgage. The fact that you don't have to utilize only cash makes purchasing rental property one of the best investment strategies in 2020 and beyond. Purchasing an investment property all in cash is difficult even for experts in real estate investing, not to mention beginners. However, you need not to worry about how to make money investing in real estate if you don't have enough funds as financing a property with a mortgage will be a reasonable alternative. The expected low interest rate is another reason why real estate investing is a good choice in 2020.

12. Housing Market Is Transforming

The real estate market has been a seller's market. While a sudden change to a buyer's market is not expected to take place in 2020, the slow transition in this direction which started in 2019 is forecast to continue. The stabilizing inventory, the slowdown in appreciation, and the low mortgage interest rates are all pointing to this real estate trend. This will be a very important positive factor, especially for beginner real estate investor who will not need to enter into bidding wars and compete with homebuyers and more experienced property investors.

So, is real estate a good investment in 2020? The obvious answer to this is YES! Real estate properties keep on heading the rundown of the top investment strategies as they enable investors to profit, both in short term and long term while keeping their day job. As a new investor, just remember to start small with a single family home or a duplex, and consider hiring a rental property manager to avoid stress and to enjoy your rental income.

Real Estate Investing For Beginners - Strategies for 2020

Do you really want to go into real estate investing to earn big in 2020? If yes, then you should follow these proven real estate strategies for beginners and professionals.

13. Spend time on Research

When deciding on real estate investing, you have to be informed about everything that has to do with real estate investing in order to make sure that the choice you make is the best. Get lots of information, from the Internet or the local newspapers and agencies, and use it productively. If real estate investing is your top priority, make sure you get a clear picture of what the property is worth at the purchase date. In case you decide to sell later, the financial side in real estate investing will tell you how prices can vary and what you should expect. Also, it is capital that you take into consideration if repairs and affiliate costs are included in the budget of real estate investing.

14. Invest enough time in Researching

When settling on real estate investing, you need to have adequate knowledge about everything that has to do with real estate investing in other to make sure that the decision you made is the best. Get loads of information. All information you can get from the Internet, and books. Use it productively. If real estate investing is your priority, ensure you get a clear picture of what the property is worth at the purchase date. If you choose to sell later, the monetary side in real estate investing will reveal to you how prices can vary, and what you should expect. Also, it is capital that you take into consideration if repairs costs are included in the budget of real estate investing.

15. Develop a game plan for each investment property

You should know beforehand what to do with a property before you purchase it. This game plan should have an exit strategy with the potential capital gains that you want to achieve before you sell. Also plan what your investment strategy and how you can achieve it.

16. Know your budget and evaluate your options

Real estate investing cannot be separated from budget evaluation. This means that you will have to get a clear picture of how much money you can spend on a certain property. The trick therefore is to establish straightforward limits for your budgets so that real estate investing won't dry your accounts. Time is another element that draws heavily on your success, so make sure you seize the moment and obtain the best offer, before anyone else gets ahead of you. Work hard to research and narrow down your options, you will find out that you can start making some serious money with real estate investing yet!

17. Compare the property and bargain down the price

Very often, real estate investing will put you in a position where two or more estates seem very promising, and the choice become difficult. This shows how important the ability of comparing the offers is for somebody who adopts real estate investing. In close connection with comparison comes the negotiation skill, which is a must for all those working in real estate investing. Just think about it; you find the perfect estate, but the price is insane.

So, negotiating may very well get that house for you without having to pay a fortune.

18. Value Adding

Real estate investing should also make you consider before buying, if you can add value to the property you wish to purchase. The trick is to learn how to do small things that can make a big increase in the property value. But this ties in with the previous point, that is you need to research to see if the current property price is worth your while and effort.

These strategies have been proven by real estate experts and they are truly effective. Taking massive action today is what you need to generate wealth in real estate investing in 2020. So seize the day, and the money that you dream of may come sooner than you think.

CHAPTER 8

BENEFITS OF REAL ESTATE INVESTING

Real estate investing is an investment decision that can generate high profits if you know what you are doing. Besides the financial gains, there are other added advantages that you can enjoy. Like increase in the personal wealth, experience and so on. Real estate investing is safe and subject to lesser fluctuation as compared to others investment. Real estate investments is at a lower risk. If you purchase an investment property, having a strategic location, it might drastically increase in value, which will yield high profits.

As a property investor, getting a loan approved is easier. So, you can keep the investment going and keep enjoying great returns altogether. Setting off on your property investment career, you can begin with a unit duplex. This way you can obtain high yields without getting into a worrisome mortgage or a huge financial responsibility. Smaller investment properties also helps in building a good investing experience, prior to buying a bigger property. Once you get the funds and experience, you can move to investing in bigger properties and take more enterprising real estate projects, like display homes or converted hotels purchases.

You can make an investment with other individuals by pooling together your funds with them. There are loads of opportunities for investing in commercial, industrial and residential properties. There is a potential for huge returns when investing in real estate. Make research on the location you are purchasing in. Plan, save, budget, and seek assistance from financial experts. This will enable you make an intelligent decision, which would produce great monetary benefits.

When the residential real estate market is on a rise, and all types of homes are selling faster than ever, why leave money to sit in your bank account when it could grow substantially by being invested in a property. Though there are some associated costs, but these get covered by the rental income, along with a judicious financial planning. In fact, the rental income itself is a durable source of income, and may provide you with more money than what you need to pay for your mortgage. It means that the surplus amount can be saved, enjoyed or used in the additional costs, associated with property ownership.

Once you purchase a property, whether big or small, getting finance from the major banks would be quite easy for you. Once you make some property investments and timely mortgage repayments, the banks would consider you as a safe and low-risk borrower. Thus, they would not take time to approve your loan application. This way, you can begin to increase your real estate investment portfolio. For better financial results, getting a piece of advice from professionals, real estate agent, and so on, can be of great help. So, go ahead and enjoy all these benefits of real estate investing.

Other real estate investment benefits includes;

1. Good Returns

In an average market, most real estate investors will see an annual return of between 8-10%. This steady increase in property values is often a lot better than what you'll earn with a money market or standard savings program.

2. Fairly Easy

Almost anyone can get into the property market at some price point, even if you only have modest means. While you may not be able to buy a penthouse in Manhattan, a small property in a rural town could fit the bill.

3. Real Estate Investing Provides Leverage

Leverage is being able to use credit to finance the purchase or development of a property investment. Because property can be used as collateral, you're able to invest in something without putting up all the cash yourself.

4. It Appreciates In The Long Run

Real estate will appreciate over the long term, and do so consistently. Unlike a tech stock or a hot mutual fund, a real estate investment will continue to appreciate.

5. Stability

Unlike a sometimes risky stock investment that may yield high returns initially, but drop like a rock later. Real estate is often a sound and stable investment. Overall, real estate is slow to fall, and slow to rise. Meaning with patience, you will make money.

6. Tax Benefits

Setting yourself up as a property investor means you can claim or deduct expenses like property improvement or upkeep to offset your investment income.

You can also defer some of your property investment income by using IRAs and 1031 Exchanges. For example, as long as the profits from your real estate investment remain in your IRA, they will be tax-deferred until you buy another.

7. Sweat Equity is Rewarded

Just because you invest in a company's stock doesn't mean you can walk into their office and start making improvements in marketing while giving their retail outlets a thorough cleaning.

On the other hand, real estate investing actually rewards sweat equity. You can paint walls, replace hardware, and invest your own elbow grease to actually improve the value of your investment.

CHAPTER 9

PROPERTY MANAGEMENT

Managing a property can be a very tough business. Monitoring all installments, meetings, fixes (repairs), and budgets can get extremely tough for anyone. A property management deals with everything that is involved with running a successive property. These trained experts can take care of every progression from ensuring payments are made on time to fixing damages that have occurred on the property.

Over the years, a lot of people ask "what is the most important thing about investing in real estate?" Some individuals assume its price, location or timing the market accurately. After several research, it has been realized that property management is the most significant piece of the investment puzzle. You can make a mistake on price, pick an unfavorable location, or hire a bad contractor, and still make profit. Higher the wrong property manager, and you can lose all your investment overnight. Do not get this wrong! Prices, location, and market timing are huge factors. With the right

72

property management in place though, you can make a mistake or experience a down turn in a market or neighborhood, and still get a reasonable return on your investment through positive cash flow. A good property manager protects your interest in the long run.

What Exactly Is Real Estate Property Management?

Real estate property management includes everything and anything related to running a rental property.

A property manager is an individual, association or an organization that handles, operates, and maintain a specific real estate property for a fee if the property owner has no enthusiasm in handling it himself. He serves as a contact between the property owner, and the occupants that lives or uses the property. This also serves as a balancing action as the manager must ensure that the property is always rented to function for the owner's and tenant's sake, and preserved ideally to maintain the satisfaction level of the occupants as great as possible.

The usual types of properties that managers typically handle on behalf of the owner are categorized in 5 groups, which are;

- Residential

- Multifamily

- Association

- Commercial, and

- Resort

The property manager's daily duties are usually dealing with the tenant's issues and concerns, repair of properties, property management, filing, and recording properties for rent, marketing properties available for rent and negotiating lease agreements between the owner and the tenant. Sometimes, managers also serve as rent collectors when the tenant falls late on payments, and arrange reports for the owner with regards to the property's status, and the allocation of tasks to third party vendors depending on the owner's requirements.

Reliant on the contractual arrangement between the owner and the manager, the manager may be obliged to be involved in handling the outsourcing of all management jobs associated with the property. This includes checking out standard property service businesses that are decent and reliable, and that will demand a reasonable rate in exchange for their services. It is actually an important skill for the manager to master to be able to protect the owner's investment in the property by reducing any extra costs.

The most crucial duty of a property manager to the owner is keeping the property occupied with tenants, maintaining a great level of occupancy at all times. Managers should evaluate the rental rates that should be charged to the tenants, and they should also increase the income being made from each property in the portfolio by doing a comparison analysis. The comparison analysis not only determine the physical variations in the subject property opposed to its competitors, but to identify the value of each feature so that the manager can conduct the needed adjustments to the subject property's rental charge, up or down, depending on the outcome.

For the tenants, property managers should guarantee the tenants a calm enjoyment of the premises. Comfort and security is one of the most crucial expectations that should be provided to the tenants to keep them satisfied. The tenant's safety is another major duty of the manager where tenants are allowed to live or work in a place that is free from any structural errors and defects or conditions that may be harmful to personal health or property.

Should Investors Manage their Own Real Estate Property?

One of the greatest concern to have in the wake of buying an investment property is how it will be managed. This makes a whole lot of sense since real estate property management covers numerous aspects crucial to the success of an investment property. Of course, property management incorporates a wide range of functions. They can be categorized into four segment, namely.

So, what precisely are these functions?

1. Finding Tenants

Having a system of getting tenants, showing the paper work will ensure consistent occupancy, and filling paperwork. Finding occupants is such a significant task, as getting a bad occupant can really affect your income and property. Good occupants is what you need, so invest your energy and time in finding them. The most ideal approach to do this is to have a well-executed screening and application process.

2. Collecting Rent

When an occupant has taken residence, the property manager must guarantee rent is gotten. Ordinarily, rent is paid online, although checks are also used to pay. While the method of payment is significant, it is much more significant to ensure that rent is paid in due time.

3. Legal Matters

Abiding by the law is an absolute necessity for real estate property management. As the land owner, you should know about these laws guiding real estate property management, for example, zoning laws that may restrict your ability to rent out. You also need to gain the proper document, which possible can incorporate standard licenses to operate or other prerequisites. Landowners should know eviction laws, in the rare possibility they should evict an occupant. Lastly, landowners need to be aware of their tax rules and the obligations regarding their income properties.

4. Maintenance

Another important part of real estate property management is maintaining the investment property. This incorporates repairs, renovations, and any inclusion to the property.

Since you know what real estate property management is all about, it's time to ask this very important question;

Should you self-manage your real estate properties or should you hire a professional management company?

Below is the comparison between these two property management methods.

Managing Your Real Estate Properties by Yourself

The most preferred advantage self-management has over professional management is the capacity to set aside cash. Management costs for a normal investment property are as a rule around 3 to 5 percentage of the rental revenue. While Professional property management can eat up 10 percent of your rental revenue. A few organizations even request the whole first month's rent for new occupants!

Not all the benefits of self-management are financial. One is a significant intangible "experience". Regardless of whether you plan to self-manage your investment properties, it is imperative to comprehend the rudiments of property management. What's more, there's no preferred method to do that than participating in this management. That just that, having experienced, intricate details of real estate property management property management will assist you with assessing a management organization if you desire to hire one.

Another advantage you gain with self-management is total control over your properties. You don't have to depend on anyone, or double check someone's work. This also includes the previous point gaining experience. Having more involvement and responsibility towards your rental will help you in the future if you invest in more properties.

Hiring Professional Property Management

Self-managing your investment properties can save you cash, but contracting a professional property management will save you time. The additional expenses of professional real estate property management can be justified if you have enough money available. The additional time you get can enable you to invest in multiple properties, expanding your real estate investment portfolio, and increasing your rental income.

Not only will professional property management save you time, it will also save you from stress. The stress in the real estate investing business arises from management obligations.

To have these duties dealt with by an organization will lessen your general task and stress.

Property management services are able to help with what is called association management. Association management works through everything that has to do with the association that the property is involved in. These association services include things like attending board meetings, and making recommendations for the board. The managers will also work with contracting maintenance, additions, improvements, and repairs that the property needs. The specially hired managers are able to take care of all the essential needs that any community or property needs.

Another property management service that is available is financial management services. A financial management service takes care of all things that deals with making sure bills are paid and budgets are in accordance. The hiring of these mangers will consist of them performing duties like collecting the community homeowner's fees, do assessments and collect late fees. Along with all the above listed that are part of the manager's duties. They also do things like prepare financial statements for the board's monthly meetings, and end of the year financial statements.

Property management services cover everything that has to do with your community, financially or within the homeowner's association itself. They also offer another service that can be classified as priceless, being that they are there for you anytime you need them. Especially, in the case of an emergency. Whether a water pipe bursts or your roof has a leak, they are able to help you 24 hours a day, 365 days a year. They also assist you with helping to get the damage to your property repaired as quickly as possible.

The services performed by these master managers will be able to take care of all your homeowner association needs, whether it is keeping everything in order with the property itself, or keeping all the budgets in order. A property management service takes care of everything that must be done to run a successful and effective community or property.

All management obligations take some experience and aptitude to perfect. With professional property management, you get assistance from experts. These experts assist you with facilitating management features. For instance, real estate investors fill vacancies quicker with the help of organization management. That is not all, management organizations locate the best occupants available, with the help of their detailed screenings and applications. Professional real estate property management is also very beneficial with regards to the legal aspects of property management.

In general, professional property management will assist with anything related to management, at high and precise levels.

Do You Manage on Your Own or to Hire Property Management?

Now, you know the two types of real estate property management, but which one should you adopt? The appropriate response isn't crystal clear, sadly. However, you can choose how you need your management based on your objectives and your kind of investment.

Utilizing professional property management can work property whether you plan on investing full time or part time. Notwithstanding, if you somehow happen to employ property management, it is wiser to do so while investing full time. A good example is of a real estate investor with multi-family properties, similar to an apartment. In this case, the property manager is answerable to all the units. What's more, since multi-family properties produce high income, the expenses of professional property management become tolerable.

Single family properties are likewise appropriate for professional property management. The difference is that an individual SFR (Single Family Residential) may not produce as much as a multi-family property. Thus, the expenses of professional management take a harder shot. In this case, self-management would be the better investment decision. If you have multiple SFRs, professional management can work out.

If your investment is an Airbnb property, you could likewise settle for self-managing. Airbnb investments can be very flexible, from the perfect passive investment to a full time commitment. A passive Airbnb investment could warrant self-management. An active one could utilize either type of management.

Owning a single property does not mean you can't utilize professional property management. All it implies it that the expense might be more significant than you anticipated. To avoid this, set aside some additional money before you invest in a property. This reserve could be utilized to pay professional management costs for the beginning of the investment, at least.

Should investors manage their own real estate property?

The answer to this question depends on the investor. However, self-management is more reasonable when the investor has a single income property. Especially, if it is a passive investment.

Strategies for Being a Great Property Manager

If you are focused on becoming a real estate investor, and getting renters to pay your mortgage, then you will want to perfect becoming a property manager. After all, nothing beats Cash Flow Apartment Buildings as a good real estate investment. But, to maintain good income, you must know the legal prerequisites. No two states have the same regulations. Your choices should be top notch, and you need to ensure that you have a system in place for doing such. Do it right, and for the greater degree it's going to be a fantastic experience, and will inspire you to obtain a lot more rental real estate.

Know your legal requirements for your state or province, such as how frequently are you able to increase rents, and is there a limit on the increase? Google the Tenancy Act for your region is an excellent start. You will require quality tenancy forms intended for applications, rental or lease contracts and move-in/move-out reports. There could possibly be a

Property Professionals organization in your town that you can register with. Definitely worth it, who will provide guidance along with a library of forms.

You must discover ways to choose top quality renters. A smart technique when showing potential tenants the accommodation is to arrange the showing for everyone simultaneously. This can create some urgency as they definitely will be aware there's competition for the home. Make sure you've got applications along with you at the showing to give out to the interested persons, and make sure they know you will definitely get back to all of them. Do not pick the new renter till you have checked them out! Where allowed, you will want to carry out credit rating checks and get in touch with earlier Landlords, but not their present one as she might be very happy to get free of them, and not provide you with the straight goods! In addition, you shouldn't be reluctant to "trust your gut", when a little something just isn't sitting right with you regarding the tenant, despite the fact that everything checked out nicely, do not rent to them and proceed to the next!

You must get a full process set up. For instance, retaining individual files for every property. Know where you should advertise. For rent sign on the property, ad in classifieds, post at the local college or university, or website such as Craigslist are the ideal methods for locating renters. You should establish a list of excellent trades persons intended for painting, electrical, plumbing, window & gutter cleaning, etc. One of the very first items you ought to do with a brand new property is have all the locks re-keyed so you have one master key for your own benefit. Practically, nothing is much more irritating than having a pants pocket filled with keys for one property and trying determine which key fits just what!

Do not forget that owning rental properties is a business, so address it as such. Get to understand your legal obligations, pick top quality renters and get a system in place. Learn how to be a great property manager, and you'll land excellent tenants almost every time. They will pay off your mortgage loan on your behalf, thereby making you wealthy.

There is a lot to learn about property investments and management for beginners. The following are few things you need to know;

- **Start With Searching for Investment Properties**

  There are plenty of ways to look for investment properties. You can find them through classified ads and online. To make the search faster and easier for you, you may need to get the assistance of an estate agent who is much more knowledgeable, and has the proper connections to get access to commercial, and other income generating estates.

- **Consider Accessibility and Convenience**

In your search for investment properties, you need to consider several factors. This factors includes the convenience of the site. There are several advantages to a property that is close to shops, parks, transportation and an overall safe neighborhood.

This can affect the demand of the rental. You have to consider tenant's needs, and make sure you invest in properties with those needs. It is also in your best interest to get adequate information, understand and be knowledgeable about certain restrictions that may have an impact on the rental agreement.

- **Consider improving the property**

Assess the condition of the property. In this regard, the service of a property inspector is crucial. He can help you find areas that absolutely need improvements, and can give you an idea about possible repair costs. In this way, your decision can be much more guided knowing exactly what condition the structure is in.

- **New Versus Old Properties**

It can be especially expensive to buy a new home so if you are after bargain prices, you would want to browse through older property listings. Be careful however when going for this option. Although the cost of the purchase may be much lower, you may need to spend a lot of repair which would defeat your very purpose of buying inexpensively.

At best, you should set proper expectations by knowing beforehand, how much repair and maintenance would cost. This way, you can make proper estimates, and decide whether the property is worth the cost it is being asked for. To get to know this for sure, an inspector and an appraiser can be of great help in determining the fair and real market value of the property.

There are other important factors to your decision making, and you have to make it a point to get to know and master those aspects as well.

CHAPTER 10

REAL ESTATE INVESTING FOR BEGINNERS – FREQUENTLY ASKED QUESTIONS (FAQ)

These chapter will answer every possible questions you might want to ask about real estate investing for beginners.

How do I start investing in real estate?

1. Write down your objectives. Be explicit.

2. Pick the kind of property to invest in. There are numerous choices when starting as a new investor.

3. Find out your financial requirements.

4. Get a partner. (This is optional)

5. Choose an area or location

6. Search for a property.

7. Make offers.

Is real estate a wise investment in 2020?

Generally, markets with high level of growth are preferred wagers over those with lower growth rate, yet a steady growth rate is just as significant in the long run. Even with interest rates rising, investing in real estate will definitely be a great move in 2020.

How do I kick-start investing in real estate with little cash?

There are a lot of ways to start investing in real estate with little or no cash, but this is considered the best method.

Simply purchase a home as primary residence. You can simply buy a home to live in with a zero down VA or USDA loan, remain there for at least one year, and afterward move out, and transform the home into an investment property. Keep in mind that equity building through real estate investing incorporates the homes in which you live.

How much money do you need to kick start investing in real estate?

In general, real estate investment partnerships normally take an investment between the range of 5000USD and 50000USD. While 5000USD isn't sufficient to buy a unit in the normal building, several partnership exist that pull cash from different financial specialists to buy a property that is shared and co-owned by several investors.

Is Real Estate Investing worth it?

Real estate is an extraordinary investment that can generate a progressive passive income. It can be a good long term investment if the value increases over time. For one, you should put down a reasonable amount of cash upfront to begin real estate investing.

How does a real estate investment work to create wealth?

Wealth is created through longer real estate investing strategies, which includes purchasing and holding property. In this situation, the investor purchases a property and afterward, leases it to an occupant or leases it to an occupant with the option to purchase.

How can I make the most money in real estate?

1. Long term residential rentals. One of the most widely recognized techniques for profiting in real estate is to leverage long-term purchase and hold residential rentals.

91

2. Lease option

3. Short sales

4. Contract flipping

5. Commercial real estate

6. Home-renovation flips

7. Hard-money lending

8. Vacation rentals

What are the types of Real Estate?

The most widely recognized class is single-family homes. There are also apartment suites, centers, duplexes, triple-deckers, high-value homes, multi-generational, and vacation homes.

What are the types of property?

There are three wide types of property; private property, public, and collective property (Collective property is also called cooperative property)

What makes a good property manager?

A property manager should be able to listen and communicate. As well as be proactive and involved, current, and educated (knowledgeable). The person needs to be reasonable, creative, and understandable.

What are the prerequisites to become a property manager?

Property renting managers need at least a high school (secondary school) diploma, and some employers prefer applicants with a college degree in a relevant field such as; business administration, real estate, finance, accounting or public administration. Most employers search for candidates with 1-5 years of working experience.

Can I go into property management without a license?

Property managers are required to hold a property management license or a real estate broker's license in order to conduct real estate transactions, which incorporates those related with managing and renting investment properties. However, some states do not have this requirement.

How much does a property manager make hourly?

The average hourly rate for residential property manager ranges from $24 to $31 with the average hourly pay of $28.

What skills do I need to possess for property management?

There a certain skills that all property managers need

- A property manager or company needs strong communication.

- A property managers to be exceptionally organized.

- A property managers must exemplify responsive customer service.

- A Property manager or company needs to have hands-on skills.

- Property managers need to know the basics of marketing.

How do I get started in property management?

- Know the laws guiding property management.

- Begin with small, targeted work.

- Employ the right people.

- Determine your pricing.

- Set up internal processes.

- Find rental property management software.

- Find your first tenants.

Can you write off property management fees?

Are property management charges paid to an organization for a rental property tax deductible? Yes, you can deduct management fees for your rental.

CHAPTER 11

GETTING STARTED IN REAL ESTATE INVESTING

You want to start investing in real estate, but you are not just sure what you need, how much money does it take? What sort of financial condition do you need to be in?

What should be your goal?

What's real estate time frame?

Is a particular mindset useful or even necessary?

All these are reasonable questions to ask. After all, you don't want to dive into a pool until you are sure how deep the water is.

Similarly, you shouldn't dive into real estate investing until you have planned the financial debts involved.

How much money do I need?

Not a whole lot. Of course the amount depends on where you are starting. If you are to buy your first rental house, and if you are willing to move into it for a while before you subsequently rent it out and resale it, then the very best financing in the world is available to you. You can get a mortgage for as small as 3% of the purchase price. That means you can get financing to cover all of the cost of the home plus virtually all of the cost of the closing. Your other pocket expenses are zero. How else can you get into an investment for as little? Of course it is a different story if you buy a home with the express intentions of using it as an investment rental. You'll need to put about 10% down, plus closing cost. On a $200000 home, that's about $25000, a substantial sum of money.

Should I Invest Full time?

In the beginning, it's usually a mistake to invest in real estate as a full time job. For most people, the best way to invest in property is usually on a part time basis. It is important to understand that initially, it is unlikely that you'll get enough income to live on out of your properties. After a few year, when the property have aged, values, and rental has gone up, it's a different story. But for the first ten years, it's better to think in terms of reinvesting rather than withdrawing income.

All of which is to say you need to have a steady old time job for at least, the first ten years you are investing, because your property won't likely yield enough steady income for you to live on. The most successful real estate investors in the world buy property for the long-term. If you go the long term route, you won't have to worry about occasional making mistakes, because property values always go up with inflation and housing scarcity. So, eventually you'll come out alright.

Aiming at first, just to break even, most investors don't count on taking money out monthly. After a few years however, when rental rate goes up, they will probably be able to take out a strong steady stream of income.

So consider investing in real estate on this side. For a while at least, don't make it your primary objective. This implies that you shouldn't quit your day job. Just keep at it for enough years, and you'll be able to retire early with a huge bounty to rely on.

You should plan on holding real estate investment for a long-term, because you are building your net worth. The more property you own, presumably the more your wealth over time. And also, because this wealth tends to be liquid, in the span of a few years, you might easily acquire a million dollars or more in property, but you will probably have very little cash in the bank. This situation is being spoken of as being cash poor. A common condition for real estate investors. Being cash-poor however, is no longer the serious problem that it was in recent years. Today, with equity loans and all refinancing possible, it's easier to get cash out of your investing property when you need it. All of which is to say that if you own a lot of property, and have a suddenly personal expense, you'll probably have the means to easily cover it. For instance, let's assume a big personal expense comes up such as sudden illness, a wedding, college education, or the need for a new car. Anything that requires a lot of money. To get the money you need, you can refinance a property. Alternatively, you can resell a property. But that will take more time and you'll no longer have your investment.

Some financial advisers will advise young couples to put away a certain percentage of their income, usually into stocks and bonds, which these advisers often just happen to be selling, so that the couple will have the money to pay for their children's education and their own retirement. This philosophy seem to be that you should live less well today, by scrimping and saving so that you can live less well tomorrow. How much better is it to own a bunch of home and other real estate, nearly paid off that you can harvest the money you need for these expenses, when you need it. And you don't have to be scrimping and saving your entire live to pay for these expenses. Your tenants will handle that for you.

What's my time frame? Or how long will it take to make my fortune in real estate?

The answer is figure on as much as ten years or more. Twenty years is ideal. You may be lucky and come across series of properties that you flip, split, subdivide one property into two, thus doubling your money or otherwise, well for a big profit. But depending on that is like gambling on a lottery. It's greater that comes in, but do not count on it. Instead rely on the slow and steady and sure.

Think of it in simple terms. Planning on buying one house every year or two for twenty years. At the end of that time, you'll own 10-20 houses. The first house will be roughly half paid off, the return on equity from a mortgage is the greatest in the last years, the least in the first years. Thus, after paying two-third of the time on the mortgage, the house will be roughly only half paid off. Further, inflation and housing shortages likely we will make that first house 2-3 times what you paid for it, no matter what you paid for it. Chances are that by the end of that twenty years period, you will have a million dollars or more in equity that you can convert to cash if you need to. In addition, you will have positive cash flow as well. Remember, rental rates on those early property will go up because of inflation and national housing shortages in many areas, just as prices do. You will be renting them for 2-3 times the original rent, even though your mortgage payment will be roughly the same to when you started, assuming you haven't refinanced. All of which is to say that in addition to having a large net worth, you will also have a large monthly income overtime. This is the point where you can retire from your regular job and live off your properties. Remember, we are not talking about doing something difficult, we are talking about buying one property every year or two, for twenty years. What could be simpler? Of course, there may be obstacles, you could have a bad year and lose your job for a time, but even if that happens, while you might not be able to buy a new home that year, you'll have the homes you already own to fall back upon. Of course, those who see the glasses always half empty will say you could get sick or die, or the economy could lose dive. Yes, those things could happen, but they are going to happen whether or not you invest in real estate. So, why not invest and hope for the best?

What Mindset Do I Need To Become a Successful Investor?

There is really only one requirement; that you understand the difference between your business and your personal life. When buying a home for investment, you will feel countless thugs against your better judgement to buy a property, because it offers so many pleasing features. You may love the layout of the kitchen, the tile in the bathroom. It can be adorable, the backyard may be perfect for your family. The garage is ideal because it is big with lots of storage space, plus there is a work bench. All of the above will be good reasons to select a home for your personal life. A home that will be best suited to your taste, needs and desire. However, when buying investment property, you need to put all that aside and let the reasoning portion of your mind take over. You need to be all business. The questions to ask are;

Will these feature or that one be suitable for tenants?

Is it easily replaced if it is damaged or destroyed?

Will the feature make the house more or less sellable in the future?

You have to put aside all personal feelings when you consider the property. You must be strictly business. This also applies when it comes to money. When it's time to buy or sell a property, you must go for the very best deal possible. You can't let yourself be swayed by feeling sorry for the other person's situation. For instance, tenants may tell you that they can't or won't pay their rents because they have some other bills. You have to be strong enough to tell them that the rent comes first and demand immediate payment. If you act weak to a tenant's problem, it then becomes your problem, because you don't have the rental money with which to pay your bills.

Similarly, when negotiating for the purchase or sale of a home, you may find that you are dealing with people with a lot of personal problems, from illness, to divorce, to bankruptcy. Your heart may go out to them. However, the way you help them is not to make their problem yours by paying too much or selling for too little. It's by removing a problem from them. For instance, you can help a person who is destined to lose his or her house to foreclosure by buying it from them, which will help to save their credit. If you want to go further and give the money to get them back on their feet, you should be applauded. However, be sure you understand your motivation, getting their home out of foreclosure was business, helping them is charity. Both are admirable, but it is important not to confuse one with the other.

What Other Quality Do I Need to Be Successful?

Do a successful real estate investor needs to have a mind that pays attention to detail? The answer is YES. But then again, it's hard to imagine that any line of endeavor where lack of attention to detail is an asset. You'll find that you need to keep track of market values, rental payments, and all sorts of numbers. A good ledger will help, but it's still up to you to remember the details.

You might also want to ask. Do you have to be a "people-person" to make a good real estate investor? Again, it's hard to imagine any line of work where personal interactions aren't important. However, in real estate investing, they can be less important than elsewhere. You don't need to sell yourself to purchase investment property or to be a landlord. Although, a pleasing personality and the determination to deal fairly with people are great assets here and elsewhere. In this business, many successful real estate investors are reclusive. You almost never see them, and when you do, they don't have ten words to say. On the other hand, if you intend to sell a property on your own, then it helps to be gregarious in nature. You'll be dealing directly with potential buyers, and if you have an ability to chat and make friends easily, it will help. Of course, you don't have to sell on your own because you can always sell through an agent. Thus, it turns out that you don't need a lot of money to get started. But you do need determination and the ability to separate your business from your personal life. You also need to understand that you are in it for a long term. So, don't quit your day job. At least, not right away.

Mistakes to Avoid in Real Estate Investing

The possibility of profiting from real estate investment is very appealing. However, one needs to realize that there is the enormous duty of learning the ins and outs of the industry so as to profit and not make lose. Beginners in real estate investment must have the knowledge about mistakes he can possibly make, with the goal that he can avoid making such mistakes and find real estate investment a beneficial activity that brings in the desired profit.

Years of experience in real estate investment is a good thing, but they do not guarantee one of expertise. For the new investor, there is a greater need to learn and educate oneself, especially since he must first master the essential guidelines of investing.

While it is true that real estate is a very good investment, you should be careful when your purchase a property. Do not plunge ahead without carefully studying the property and the current market trends. There are different kinds of real estate investment and all of them have their pros and cons.

There is a ton of mistakes that can be made in real estate investment. Many professional investor still commit errors or have overcome enormous mistakes in their investing careers.

The following are some helpful points that can guide a newbie investor.

1. Buying too many properties in a short time. Avoid the mistake of buying too many real estate properties too soon. If this mistake is done, then an investor can have his resources spread out too thin and in the process, he can become too overwhelmed with the associated expenses and responsibilities.

2. Mortgaging too much money on the property. This is the same as leveraging too much money on a commercial real estate. Make sure that you can afford the home you wish to buy, not buy a home that you want to be able to afford.

3. Not paying the right taxes. We all know that any real estate property requires the payment of some taxes. Never allow your tax arrears to pile up so you would not have to wake up one day with too much money

owed to the government. It is best that you get a good and trustworthy tax adviser and accountant right at the very start of your business.

4. Inappropriate Analysis of Property. A commercial property that appears great outside might have damage and other problems on the inside and vice versa. Have it appraised by professionals and take time to research the title. See to it that taxes are up to date and ask a contractor or a mechanic to give you an estimate for possible repairs. It is also good to be aware of any zoning limitations.

5. Paying too much for a piece of property. One mistake to avoid is to pay too high a price for a property. It is important to understand that you must also make money from buying and not just from selling it in the future. Purchase your property at the right price and then add force appreciation into it. In the end, you can make good money now and in the future.

6. Crunching the wrong numbers when you try to find out if it is a solid investment or not. You should look at the up-front costs of purchasing the property that also includes closing costs, taxes, appraisals and title

work. Repair costs, upgrades and replacements should also be considered. If it comes out more costly than the income you get from it, then it is a bad investment. Try to think ahead and ask yourself if there would be problems arising later on that prevent you from making money. How long it takes a similar property to sell.

7. Not getting reinvestment. It would also be a huge mistake not to make necessary reinvestment. Never be too tight-fisted that you do not make necessary repairs on your properties, for instance. If you fail to repair things in your rented property, for example, you can simply end up with a liability that can drain your finances more. Also, leaving your property in a bad condition can make your tenants feel the same way as well - they won't give importance to what you have invested in.

8. Unable to analyze the market. Take note that in a commercial real estate investment, the market is far more important than the property. Be sure to analyze the market thoroughly before you invest.

9. Not having a management system. It can be a huge mistake not to systematically keep track of your property investments. Thus, having a good management system is necessary. Be sure that you understand and monitor investments, tax records, developments, and the money flow.

10. Failing to be pre-approved before you hunt for a house. Pre-approval tells where you are financially and can prevent you from looking at homes you cannot afford. A pre-approval also tells your mortgage lender that you are ready and reveals to a home seller that you are serious in making the purchase. Pre-approval helps speed up the buying process.

11. One of the biggest mistakes is failing to check on your credit report before applying for a mortgage. When you apply for a mortgage, you are entitled to have a copy of your credit report. This check is called the 'soft pull', and does not show up on your report. Take the time to check it so that you can remove any discrepancies prior to applying for a home mortgage.

12. Jumping in deep without a clear plan of action. Do not dive right into any kind of investment without you

doing thorough research first. Make sure that you have looked into all the angles of the said investment. Also, it is important that you set clear immediate and long-term goals. If you do not plan ahead, then you might as well be planning to fail.

13. First-time home-buyers do not know about first time home-buyer programs available. These incentives can save you money by reducing the amount of your down payment. They can also help you get a loan approved if you have sub-par credit. Look at all possibilities and options before you make a choice. Discuss your plans with a professional and choose a program that will give you the most benefit.

14. Borrowing too much money to purchase. You must take into account that if you borrow too much in order to purchase a property, the interest would be sky high. In the beginning where profits are slow, you might find difficulty paying off your loan and the interest.

15. Becoming a know-it-all. In real estate property investments, things like market and prices always change. Never become too confident especially since

you need to learn and research continually. In order to get ahead in the investment business, you need to understand and go with the changes as needed.

There are many other mistakes that an amateur investor can commit. You need to be very sure that you do not make the mistakes listed above, so you can avoid wasting money, effort, and time. You also need to keep learning and researching, especially when it comes to potential investments.

CHAPTER 12

FINDING GOOD INVESTMENT PROPERTIES

There are over 65million homes in the Unites States, and the vast majority are singe family dwellings. For a new investor, this inventory represent a huge treasure trove of getting started properties. They are everywhere, to find the best one for you, you just have to know how to sift through the pile. Before jumping in however, it is important to clearly define what we are looking for. A house makes a great first investment. Probably the best. However, it's not just any house we want, it's a house we can make a profit on. That means we must be able to buy it inexpensively. The ideal investment property will sell for below the market price. Where do we find it?

There are five areas to be considered.

1. Property listed with local agents

2. Property listed as for sale by owner

3. Property listed on the internet

4. Foreclosures and property listed as real estate owned

5. Government repose

In any endeavor, it is important to take advantage of what is already out there to help you. Already in place is a vast network of listed properties. Indeed, at any given time, probably around 85% of the property for sale are listed with agents. So, the first step is to tap into this resource.

Many beginning investors say something like "There is nothing good listed". "If there were, an investor or agent would have already bought it". That's a mistake in thinking. Normally, there are so many properties for sale at any given time that there are bargains out there that are just waiting to be discovered.

Further, every agent would much rather get a commission, which means immediate income. Then buy a listed property, which means a long term investment. Agents need that constant influxive cash that commission supply to survive. Normally, they buy for investment only as a last resort. All of which is to say that, the person who complains about the lack of bargains and listings probably hasn't taken the time to look. Only after you have spent a month or two, checking out all currently listed properties in your area should you conclude that there is nothing for you in the Multiple Listing Service (MLS).

You want to work with an agent who have access to the Multiple Listing Service in your area.

Agents who have access are usually members of the National Association of Realtors. Tell your agent exactly what you are interested in. If you are just getting started, you might be looking for a house both as a place to live and as an investment. You have your choice of the greatest selection of properties on the MLS.

Look for stale listings.

Stale properties are those that have been listed the longest. A seller who put his property on the market on Monday isn't likely to cut his or her price by Friday. On the other hand, a seller who's had his property on the market for three months with no activity is likely to be very anxious to make a deal and cut his or her price to do it. In a normal market, a large number of properties will be in the stale category. Indeed, most property will take two months or more to sell. In a slow market, you'll want to extend your time frame to homes that have gone unsold for six months or longer. In a hot market however, you'll have to reduce that time frame, sometimes to a few weeks.

Look for Price reductions.

Another indication that a seller is anxious to dump a property is a price reduction. Particularly, a large reduction. A seller who cuts the price by $1000 is merely trying to attract attention. A seller who cuts the price by $10,000 is serious. Multiple price reductions, particularly when they come in close succession indicate a very anxious seller. When you find a property that has been reduced in price, and that otherwise seem suitable. Don't feel you have to offer the current asking price. Just because a seller has reduced the price doesn't mean the price is at rock bottom. Treat a reduced price as you would any other. The starting point for negotiations work down from there.

Check for clues in the listings.

Listing agents have a duty to protect their clients. In this case, the sellers. And they must do everything they can to attract buyers. This means letting buyers know when sellers are highly motivated to sell, which they accomplish often by writing clues into the listing. Look for phrases such as "highly motivated" or "bring in all offers" or "wants to move immediately". The agents is sending out the word that this seller is very anxious and will consider low offers. If the property is also listed with price reductions, you probably have a real opportunity in the making.

Check out the properties.

While this may seem simple minded, the fact is some beginner investors prefer the paper work. They will find a property that looks terrific on paper and make an offer. Real estate property are not homogenous. That means that every property has unique characteristics. No matter how good a property looks on paper, you have to check it out physically before you make an offer for it. You might find that this terrific property backs up to a dump-site, or have high tension electric wire travelling over the fence line, or the street in front is all broken up and the city have no plans to fix it. Nothing takes the place of looking at a property.

There are advantages to buying a property close to where you work. Think of this area as your farm. You'll define certain neighborhood as good investment areas and on a fairly regular basis, drive or walk through. Look for signs that indicate a person is selling his or her home. When you find a property that look suitable based on the criteria at the beginning of this chapter, start buying and engage the seller/owner in discussion. Find out what the asking price is and if there are any special features. Then check it out. Do a Comparative Market Analysis (CMA). You might find that the price is high or even higher than the market price. How can a seller even think that? The reason the price is so high is that most sellers don't think about the work involved in selling their property as much as they do about saving a big commission. Hence, they price their homes unrealistically. You will occasionally find a property seller who sees the light. He or she has prices his or her home below market in other to attract buyers, rather than attempt to save commission. This seller will give the commission to the buyer in the form of a lower price, in other to get a faster sale. This is someone with whom you can reason and negotiate. This is not to say that you should immediately pay the full asking price, even if it is below market. You should still negotiate. But, it is better to start with a realistic seller, than a seller who think that her property is so wonderful that you are to pay full price for it.

Foreclosures and REOs

Everyone has heard about foreclosures. For which an owner loses his or her property to the lender, usually for non-payment of the mortgage. Most people also have heard that if you can pick up a property in foreclosure, you stand to make a good profit. What few people have heard of however, are REOs. These are properties that have gone through the foreclosure process, are now owned by the bank, and they are for sale from the bank.

We'll discuss Foreclosures and REOs, to see where there is opportunity fr investors.

Foreclosures;

Step 1 – The seller can't or won't make payment for whatever reason and the lender puts the mortgage in default.

Step 2 – After a legally determined period of time, the lender sells the property to the highest bidder on the court house steps.

Step 3 – Typically, the lender is the highest bidder. He takes control of the property and attempts to resale it as a real estate owned property (REO).

The seller can't or make the mortgage payment. He or she is motivated to sell the property, hoping to save a credit rating. This seller is going to at least listen to any offer that you make. In a strong market, when we think that there simply aren't any seller in foreclosure, that is simply not the case. The foreclosure rate in good times may be half what it is in bad times. But in anytime, there are still plenty of foreclosures. Sellers are always losing property. Some of the more common reasons include the following;

The Seller has over borrowed and can't make the payments.

There is an illness, death, or divorce in the family and no one takes charge of maintaining the property, allowing it to fall through the cracks into foreclosure. The seller moved and listed the house, but the agent was terrible and no buyer was found. Now, the seller, at a distance just won't or can't deal with the house anymore. The seller doesn't just simply care about the property. Rare, but it does happen.

Finding Foreclosures

There are many sources of foreclosures listings. Sometimes, property listed with an agent will be in foreclosure. If you find one of these, you know you are dealing with a motivated seller.

Sources of foreclosures include; Title insurance company, who act as trustees in foreclosures. The will often provide a list of foreclosures they are handling. In addition, there is always a local legal newspaper. One that carries legal notices, in which foreclosure notices are published. Pick this up and you probably will be able to find every foreclosure in town. Be aware however, that frequently only the legal description of the property is given, not the street address. You can get the legal description translated at the county assessor's office, but doing so can be a hassle. Also, most large metropolitan areas have a foreclosure bulletin. These is a private publication that list all foreclosures. It gives street addresses, names, dates and so on. It's everything you need. However, it usually cost a lot. Typically, several hundred dollars yearly to subscribe.

Finally, a number of websites deal almost exclusively in foreclosures and REOs. When using any site however, be sure to check that the foreclosure is indeed in your area. Once you find someone who is in foreclosure, it is then up to you to contact him or her directly and find out if there is a good deal available for you. Hopefully, you already have a name and phone number. Now, just give this person a call and explain that you are an investor and you are looking for property in the area. You heard he or she was having difficulty in making payments and you are wondering if there is a way to make a win-win situation out of it. The seller gets to save his or her credit plus perhaps, some money depending on the seller's equity, and you get the property. What you can offer to the owner is to make up the back payment and penalties, and save the owner credit ratings in exchange for the titles to the property. In other words, you can offer to take it over. The advantage here is that you get the property for virtually no money down plus whatever equity the owner may have. The disadvantage is that the loan may not be assumable. If that's the case, you may not only have to make a back payment and penalties, but also secure a new loan with accompanying fees. In short, it may cost you thousands of dollars to take over this property and bail out this owner. You may find out that by the time you add up the cost, it simply isn't worth the while. It is important that you calculate these costs as accurately as possible before you make any kind of offer to the owner. You may find that it isn't simply worth your time to attempt to write a foreclosure and overtake the property.

Real Estate Owned (REO)

REO refers to property that a lenders has taken back through foreclosures. Lenders hate this kind of properties, because on their book, it shows up as a liability instead of as an asset. Therefore, they are very anxious to get rid of it. However, they are not so anxious that they are willing to take a loss, if there is any way to avert it. There is a big advantage for a buyer dealing with a lender rather than a home seller in foreclosure. It's a clean deal with the bank. There is no crime or recriminations. Also, you can get title insurance, and sometimes the bank will even help you with the financing. In fact, REOs can be a wonderful opportunity. The trick is finding out about them. Strangely, most lenders won't admit publicly, that they have an REO problem. Many won't admit they even have any REOs. Thus, you can't usually just walk and ask to buy one. This secrecy certainly seem to work against the lenders best interest, at least on the surface. One will think that the lender will be out there advertising those properties as heavily as possible, yet the lender doesn't. Do you ever recall seeing a lender advertising under its own name for REO buyers? It usually just doesn't happen. Most of the public isn't even familiar with the term REO. The reasoning of the lenders is three folds, as follows;

1. A lender doesn't want to alert federal watch dogs that he has an REO problem. Keeping up a good face can mean the difference between considered to be in business or insolvent.

2. Depositors are wary about where they place their money. Yes, we know every account is guaranteed to $100,000, but how many of us want to put that guarantee to the test? We might bolt if we thought that

the lender was shaky. In addition, there are holders of amounts larger than $100,000 who frequently move funds, lender to lender, in an effort to tie up the highest interest rates. These large depositors are not insured and they will pull their funds at the slightest sign of trouble from a lending institution. Hence, lenders are very careful not to admit they have many REOs, if for no other reason than to protect their own image.

3. There is the matter of the real estate market. If it were to be widely known that the lender had an overhang of homes, ready to dump on the market in a particular area. That information could adversely affect prices. This would back fire for the lender, since it will lower the prices for the property it was trying to sell.

Finding Real Estate Owned (REOs)

The truth is why lenders keep quiet about REOs as far as the general public is concerned, there are often open about them to legitimate investors. After all, they do want to sell them in other to get the money and reinvest it in a mortgage. You, as an investor therefore, have to convince the lender that you are a legitimate buyer. What you have to do to find Res is both tedious and simple. It is tedious because you have to do it over and over again for each lender. It's simple because the process is quite easy. Basically, you need to let the lender know that you are a sophisticated investor. You need to impress the lender that you understand what an REO is, and you'd like to bid on one. Once the lender understands that you are special and not part of the public only interest dim deposits, the lender will open up. At least, in a limited way. Therefore, you need to call the lender and ask for the officer who deals with REOs, then you need to make a case that you are an investor who has the means and desire to purchase.

Sometimes, you will be told that this particular lender handles all REOs to a specific real estate broker. You'll have to contact the broker. Other rimes, you'll learn that the lender handles the REOs himself and there is a list of such properties. You'll want to get the list.

Checking out the REO

It's common to find REOs in distressed condition. After all, if you were the borrower, and you are losing the house, your equity, and your credit rating, would you be anxious to keep watering the law, or to clean up when you left?

Borrowers who lose their property through foreclosure, tend to stop taking care of the property. And some actually mess up the property. Their reaction, naturally enough is anger. And since they can't really take it out on anyone personally, they typically take it out on the property.

When you get to inspect the REO, it may still be in the terrible shape in which the lender got it back, or maybe fixed up. Lenders are not fools, they know that a distressed property will get them a distressed price. On the other hand, if they fix it up, they stand to get a far better price. However, if you arrive on the spot, just as the REO is acquired, and offer to take it as it is, the lender may agree. After all, time spent fixing up the property is lost interest to the lender.

When you find an REO in distressed condition, don't turn your head away in disgust. You may not be looking at a disaster, but rather at an opportunity.

Buying an REO

Buying an REO is like buying any other property. You make an offer to a lender. If he likes your offer, you've got a deal. If he doesn't, you can try to negotiate. Most lenders prefer all cash. That way, they get rid of the property once and for all. This simply means that you have to go to a different lender to get financing. However, don't expect great financing on REOs. Typically, you'll be looking at 10% down or more, plus closing cost. On the other hand, some lenders recognize the fact that they will get less from a cash offer. So, they agree to handle the financing themselves for a higher sales price. Sometimes, they will even throw in a cash credit towards having the property fixed up. If the lender handles the financing, you will often get the benefits of a lower down payment and easier terms plus, perhaps some fix up money. On the other hand, you'll probably pay more than you would if you were buying strictly for cash.

Problem to expect when buying an REO

- **Expect Distressed Properties**

  They are more the rule, than the exception. That means you have to be very careful to check out an REO, and determine your cost to fix it up.

  Some properties are simply hopeless. A lender may give you a terrific deal on this, but beware of what you are getting.

- **As Is**

  Most REOs are sold As Is. Even if the seller has refurbished it, the lender makes no warranty to you of any kind. This means that later on, after the sale, if you discover a problem that cost $10,000 to fix, it is your headache, not the lenders'. That's why the price is cheaper.

- **Without Disclosures**

  While most states, now require seller to provide disclosure statements, this regulation may not apply to a lender who is federally chartered. This type of lender may refuse to give you any kind of disclosure statement. Except one that the federal government requires.

- **No Repairs**

  Certainly, you'll want to get a home inspection. In fact, you'll want the most thorough inspector you can find. However, don't expect the lender to do anything towards correcting problems the inspector finds. Typically, beyond basic refurbishing, most lenders will make no repairs of any kind. Even if the inspector finds safety issue. In that case, the lender may insist you sign a statement that you accept the property at your own risk.

REOs are for Profit. Sometimes, big profit. But they are certainly not without risk. It's not recommended for first time investors. But, once you've gotten your feet wet, buying and selling properties. You may find that REO are worth the challenge.

CONCLUSION

Real estate investment has proven itself to be a way to generate income. The current downturn in property prices makes real estate investing in 2020, alluring even for those who have not tried it before. With property prices at a historic reduction, any real estate investment made in 2020 is bound to fetch handsome returns if you are willing to wait for the upswing.

While location seem to be the focus for all real estate investment, the other key to maximize profit when you invest is timing. Obviously, a good location is basic to real estate investment. If you decide to Invest in a bad location, you are basically saying farewell to your investment.

A bad location is something that one can't correct later. So, ensure you look at the town planning papers, to give you a thought of future undertakings that may come up in the zone. You have to evaluate whether these future activities will improve or deteriorate the value of homes in that location. A new established school is probably going to increase the value of your property while a shopping mall might not do that.

Those who have the money to make substantial down payment as well as regular income to make the mortgage payment is at an advantage. So, examine your finances carefully to ensure that you meet these criteria before you start looking for properties to invest in. You also need to have the financial security to wait until the market rebounds, and you can cash in on your investment, making a tidy profit.

Real estate investing has many benefits. It tends to be more beneficial in 2020, due to the large demand for properties. Aside from financial advantages, real estate investing have other important benefits, which have been highlighted in chapter 8.

More millionaires have been made in real estate than in all industrial investments combined. Therefore, as a beginner, investing in real estate is an ideal way to become wealthy in 2020 and fund your retirement. However, many people who attempt to invest in real estate get stuck on income property. Building a real estate investment doesn't have to take a lifetime. Even with little or no money, you can still become a millionaire in real estate investing, and reach your financial goals. You need to take the right approach and be committed.

Making money in real estate involves more than just buying a single investment property and waiting to earn monthly income from it. For beginners in the real estate investing, you would have already realized that it takes good planning, relevant knowledge, a lot of effort, and consistency. There is no particular secret to being a successful real estate investor. You just have to be hardworking and follow the right steps, which have also been highlighted in this book.

Anyone who is serious in investing in real properties should learn the value of hard work, and the entrepreneurial character. Always look for more info wherever it is available. There are actually many lessons to be learned.